PORTFOLIO ASSESSMENT

A Handbook for
Middle Level Teachers

PORTFOLIO ASSESSMENT

A Handbook for Middle Level Teachers

by Keith Lustig

National Middle School Association
Columbus, Ohio

LB
1029
.P67
L87
1996
mm.1998

National Middle School Association
2600 Corporate Exchange Drive, Suite 370
Columbus, Ohio 43231.
NMSA   Telephone: 1-800-528-NMSA

Printed in the United States of America

ISBN 1-56090-111-X   NMSA Stock Number 1235

Library of Congress Cataloging in Publication Data

Lustig, Keith
    Portfolio assessment: a handbook for middle level teachers/ by
    Keith Lustig
        p. cm.
    Includes bibliographical references (p.).
    ISBN 1-56090-111-X (pbk.)
        1. Portfolios in education--Handbooks, manuals, etc.
    2. Educational tests and measurements--Handbooks, manuals, etc.
    3. Middle schools--Handbooks, manuals, etc. I. Title.
    LB1029.P67L87   1996
    373.12'7--dc20   96-30253
                                                          CIP

Contents

About the Author

Keith Lustig is a seventh grade language arts teacher at Hill Middle School in Naperville, Illinois. He is active professionally, is a regional consultant with the Association of Illinois Middle Level Schools, and is a frequent presenter at middle school conferences. He holds degrees in both Communications and Educational Curriculum and Instruction.

Foreword

Hammered out in the classroom, the portfolio assessment procedures presented in this down-to-earth resource come from the voice of experience. Through professional reading, personal reflection, and a lot of trial and error, Keith Lustig, an interdisciplinary team teacher, successfully incorporated portfolios as a part of his assessment program.

The guidelines and suggestions contained in this book have a ring of reality and can be applied by any teacher who is ready to move – as all teachers must – toward more informative and authentic assessment. Despite the degree to which traditional, competitive, paper and pencil-test-dominated grading has been institutionalized, the handwriting on the wall is clear. The adequate and fair assessment of student progress requires much more than a single letter or number based largely on the degree to which an individual has temporarily acquired certain discrete bits of knowledge. As measures of process as well as product are called for, portfolios will come into almost universal usage. As self-evaluation receives the attention if should, portfolios will be very much in evidence. As students are led to take more responsibility for their education, portfolios will be a major means of achieving this goal.

A portfolio system does not do everything to correct the limitations and negative aspects of traditional grading, but it is a valuable and achievable supplement to existing procedures. This book will provide the help needed to make this move toward a more authentic system of assessing student progress.

— John H. Lounsbury

Introduction

S everal years ago I sat on a district writing committee that had been given the task of bringing about the paradigm shift needed to bring about a writing-based curriculum. A major part of the committee's discussion focused on assessment and how to maintain consistency among so many teachers at several grade levels teaching so many subject areas. As our discussions continued, a colleague of mine introduced the idea of portfolio assessment. The committee agreed that this was an interesting concept but shuttered at the thought of the logistics required to implement such a program.

Being the overachiever that I am, I decided that portfolio assessment was a concept worth exploring. Jumping in with both feet, I read all I could get my hands on. When the school year began, so did my portfolio system.

I have written this handbook not as a portfolio "guru," but simply as a classroom teacher who saw the need for changes in current classroom assessment procedures. I began a portfolio system in my language arts classroom to make students more accountable for assessing their own work and to cut my paper load. Since then, I have learned much from my mistakes and have been able to make portfolios a manageable and creative means of assessing student progress.

I continue to improve through trial and error plus additional professional reading. I have educated not only myself, but also my students, their parents, and my colleagues. What I have discovered has made my job easier and changed my entire philosophy about assessing student work. I am so committed to this concept that I served on the district evaluation committee and helped create an optional portfolio component to the district's teacher evaluation plan.

This handbook provides a teacher-friendly guide for creating, instituting, and maintaining assessment portfolios. It addresses the need for changes in student assessment and how portfolios can help teachers move in this direction. It explains the philosophy and benefits of using a portfolio system as a tool to create alternative and more authentic assessments. It includes practical advice about creating and using such a system and sample forms and examples from actual classroom portfolios. The concluding section is a collection of commonly asked questions with answers.

This professional resource is intended for the teacher who is seeking a realistic and manageable approach to implementing one aspect of authentic assessment. Although it is geared to the middle-level educator, the information and techniques included can be applied at other levels. My intention is not to add more rhetoric on the subject, but rather to share my personal successes and the methods I developed for making portfolio assessment a workable and exciting approach to monitoring the growth and progress of each individual student. ▱

1. The Difference Between Grading and Evaluation

Before initiating discussion on portfolio assesment, it is advisable to develop a common vocabulary and a philosophical baseline as a foundation for the upcoming discussion. There are so many buzzwords that come and go leaving teachers unsure of exactly what various terms mean. To fully understand the differences between grading and evaluation the purposes of assessment in today's classroom should be examined.

In all classrooms the diversity of the students – mental, physical, and cultural – is a tremendous challenge for the teacher. Nowhere is this more true than at the middle level. From their thinking skills to the distractions they bring with them, no two young adolescents are on the same page at any given moment. Even though no learners are alike, the nature of the traditional system calls for the grading of students using large group assessments. These assessments most commonly take the form of tests, quizzes, and homework. The same "tool" is used to assess each "individual" student. Teachers don't consciously choose to do this; they are forced because of time constraints, expectations, and the need to arrive at a grade for the report card or progress report.

If we were to give the same student three different types or forms of assessment, a manipulative test, an objective test, and an essay test, each covering the same material, would that child score the same on each measure? The answer is obviously *no.* This point emphasizes the fact that each student learns in his/her own way and therefore should be tested in a somewhat unique way. Our job then becomes even more complex; how do we assess each learner individually recognizing his/her unique ability and style? The answer? We find several ways to evaluate his/her progress over a period of time.

If a teacher simply gives a test to a student and records that grade, the teacher has merely taken a snapshot of one moment in time. At the end of the grading period when several snapshots have been combined into a collage, each fragment still retains its individual qualities and becomes part of the final grade. What we need to do is create an album that reveals a broader view of the student over a span of time. We can thereby discover the extent of growth and change, how each student has moved from one point in time to another. We should assess students' progress as well as their current standing.

Read the statement in the triangle below.

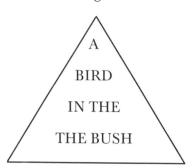

What most people see in the statement are the words "A bird in the bush." Upon closer examination, you will realize that it actually says "A bird in the the bush." The point being that both teachers and students tend to see what they expect to see. If we can begin to look at the same thing in more than one way we will begin to fill that photo album with a variety of snapshots from a variety of angles that will provide information from all sides.

Red Pensil Mentality

I would suspect that the first thing you noticed (being a good teacher) was the misspelling of the word "pencil." This is the mold teachers have been put into. This is what we are expected to do, we find the errors and point them out to the student. In fulfilling this role, what are we doing? Are we sending the right message? I don't think so. As humans we all respond with much greater enthusiasm and conviction when we are approached with positive feedback than when hit with negative correction. We need to begin focusing on the large number of letters or words that are correct rather than the one that is wrong. This begins the shift from *grading* to *evaluation*.

A portfolio might be likened to a photo album that contains a variety of snapshots. If it includes only pictures of the same pose in the same setting we would not capture the diversity that exists in our students. Therefore evaluation needs to incorporate a variety of assessments. This enables both the teacher and the student to see progress over time and helps each of them draw conclusions about strengths to utilize and weaknesses to focus on for improvement. The total picture of a student calls for information on all three levels of the assessment hierarchy.

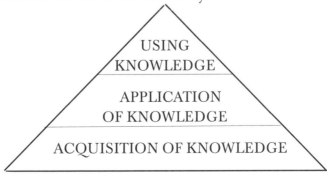

This hierarchy can be linked directly to Bloom's Taxonomy. The types of indicators you use to move up the hierarchy should be a building of knowledge one level upon another. Movement is also directly linked to the types of questions you ask. The acquisition of knowledge can be tested using literal questions. This is regurgitation testing since students are merely asked to spit back information in its basic form. By asking inferential questions students begin to apply the knowledge. They use two or more bits of literal information in order to draw a conclusion. To test the use of knowledge, ask judgmental questions. At this point students are asked to form an opinion based on a variety of information and draw conclusions that will carry over into their out-of-school lives.

Another factor that makes evaluation different from grading is assessing informal work in direct proportion to the formal work that students do. I call this the iceberg theory of assessment. I derived this concept from a seminar on writing in the language arts classroom that was directed by Ralph Fletcher (1992). During the presentation he brought forth a model that contrasts the writing students turn in with the exploratory work done to arrive at the final project. In expanding and building on this idea, I created this concept of formal vs. informal work which is applicable to all subject areas not just writing.

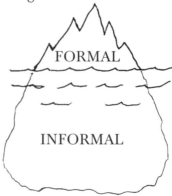

When teachers grade, they tend to keep a record only of the formal work, the work that is handed in, generally the final product. This means that the exploration or preliminary work that was done is ignored, yet it is during the exploration process that most of the learning occurs. It is also the work that consumes the most amount of time. When we only grade the final project we really aren't evaluating the learning that took place as the student moved up the assessment hierarchy. This final grade does not reflect the actual proportions of formal and informal work.

As an example, each year my students are required to do a large research paper as part of the science fair. We spend several weeks going through the research process including note taking, drafting, revising, etc. For years the majority of a student's grade was the final paper that was turned in to me. In reviewing my evaluation strategies a few years ago, I came to the realization that I was not supposed to be teaching the research *paper*, I should be teaching the research *process*. But I was assessing the paper (the formal) and not the process (the informal). By creating a new evaluation technique, a mind map, I was not only able to assess the learning of the process, I was also able to move from assessing the application of knowledge to the use of the knowledge. These mind maps are a pictorial representation of the process in the form of an analogy. Students are asked to compare the steps in the research project to the steps in some other familiar process. Usually about 8-10 pictures with brief explanations are created to compare researching to such things as planting a garden, packing for a trip, making microwave popcorn, or even studying the evolution of man. With one look, I know if the learner understood the process. The students enjoy developing mind maps, which can be graded more rapidly than a narrative account of the process. (I extend special thanks to my colleague Ann Martin for the idea.)

It is much easier to grade than to evaluate, partially because teachers haven't been taught effective and time efficient ways to evaluate. The assessment portfolio is one way to do this. The portfolio enables the teacher and student to: cooperatively work together in compiling both formal and informal examples of learning; make learning an ongoing process; and assess skills on an as-needed basis. In order for all this to take place the students must take an active role in the process. This involvement is essential as the move from grading to evaluation is made and aspects of more authentic assessment are incorporated.

As educators we must guide students toward becoming responsible for assessing their own growth. A newly emphasized goal of education is to create lifelong learners. If teachers continue to "grade" or judge students, this will not happen. Teachers must get rid of the red pencil mentality and share the responsibility for assessing with the clients. Portfolios can be a vital tool to begin this shift. 🗁

Student Reactions to Portfolio Assessment

I like this grading. I wish more teachers would do it. I tell people and they say: Ooh, Wow, Neat (like my family). I think it is great cause the teacher may or may not understand your perspective or angle. Plus you may not come up with the best ideas right away. This way you can use 20/20 hindsight for good. I can't always get a good idea but maybe when we choose a story I can add more and really clean it up. I think every teacher should do this.

I like it when we do the conferences because we can both agree on a grade so I know it was fair.

2. The Four S's of Assessment

In Chapter 1, the distinct differences between grading and evaluation were discussed. Grading tends to focus on the extent to which students have acquired knowledge, while evaluation seeks to assess how well they are applying knowledge. Teachers usually depend heavily on paper and pencil tests to gather data on their students and to have a basis for assigning a grade. In doing this they focus on a simple one-dimensional measurement, a photo of that particular moment in time. As teachers begin to evaluate, they start to place a judgment on an occurrence. This implies that there is more to look at than just an objective right or wrong answer. It is only after teachers begin to evaluate student progress that they can really assess student learning.

Assessment begins when a collection of snapshots is compiled that illustrates the process of growth and learning in students. Assessment utilizes multiple indicators to create that photo-album look at a child. This collection of data should include elements of both testing and evaluation. This variety of learning indicators leads to an evaluation of the whole. True assessment takes place when a combination of artifacts from both the formal and informal realms of student learning are examined.

An assessment portfolio is a very logical tool to use in collecting and maintaining these artifacts. Not only do portfolios provide a vehicle to track student progress over a period of time, they allow for great flexibility and creativity on the part of both student and teacher. Although portfolios encourage collaborative efforts between both parties involved, it is the teacher that ultimately must be responsible for the establishment, maintenance, and assessment of the collection.

When you begin "assessment" look long and hard at the S's in the word. You will notice that there are four of them. Each one stands for something that must be given careful consideration before entering into any true assessment program, especially one that involves portfolios. Those four S's represent *students, style, subject,* and *space.*

1. Students

As mentioned earlier, each classroom holds its own unique blend of learners. They are your clients, the reason you are there. Take a good look at them. Ask yourself: Where have they come from?, Where are they "at?" Where do they need to go? With answers to these questions you have the basis for deciding what kind of assessment system would benefit them the most.

Every student is different from every other one. This fact is part of the beauty of assessment portfolios. Each portfolio becomes a personalized collection of an individual's growth and experiences. Even though each student will compile his/her own personal and unique photo album over time, all snapshots will include similar characteristics and conditions. It is the unique but comparable backgrounds that you seek to discover and consider in your plan. Find the common threads such as culture, age, interests, and goals, then weave them in to the system you create.

While you are thinking about your students, begin to think about what things or artifacts you might want to include in their portfolios. I suggest you include items that reflect the different modalities of learning – visual, spatial, and kinesthetic. You might also wish to try utilizing Gardner's (1993) seven intelligences in your assessment plan: verbal/linguistic, mathematical/logical, musical/rhythmic, visual/spatial, body/kinesthetic, interpersonal, and intrapersonal. The more information you can compile on each learner, the more accurate will be the conclusions you draw.

2. Style

Just as every student has a unique learning style, every teacher has a unique teaching style. Take a good look at yourself. How do you run your classroom? How open are you to changing your procedures? There is no point in creating a system of assessment that won't fit into your way of doing things. This would only lead to great frustration and eventual abandonment of the program. So you must analyze how structured you are, how you feel about cooperative group work, and what is your philosophy of education. This is not an easy task, but once begun you can explore changes that will enhance your assessment techniques.

Continuing the photo album analogy, remember you are the photographer. You have ultimate control of what photographs are taken. Remember that you want as many varied snapshots as possible, so you must know yourself well enough that you can be confident when you seek a new angle to shoot the next picture. No two photographers see the exact same photo opportunity. More than likely, however, you are the only photographer on the job, so it is up to you to see a wide range of photo opportunities for each given subject. Be secure in the knowledge of yourself and your style and don't try to be something you're not when creating assessment strategies.

Your teaching style should be reflected in your assessment. You do not want to teach one way and then test or evaluate in another. Don't contrive new evaluations just to have something to place in the portfolio. Expand and revise what you currently do in order to see new sides of your students.

3. Subject

In the quest to chart the individual progress of each student you cannot forget your responsibility for assuring proficiency in acquiring basic knowledge. No two subject areas can be assessed in exactly the same way. As you contemplate your assessment portfolios think about the unique qualities of your particular subject area. Those qualities will help you choose the correct assessment tools. The type of camera and film you use depends on the photo you want at that moment.

Even though some subjects such as math or science lend themselves to a more objective testing of material, the teacher must still move the learners up the assessment hierarchy. There is little material that does the learner any good unless it helps to move to the "use of knowledge" level. Teachers of all subject areas must stretch to incorporate a variety of photos in order to assess student progress adequately.

A thoughtful look at the curriculum in any subject area will reveal a number of activities and processes that can be used as means of providing data for assessment. The trick is to seek ways to show how the information can be used and transferred into the world outside school and/or other classes.

4. Space

Space in which to keep portfolio collections can become a major issue for many teachers. This consideration has to be dealt with when creating your system. In the perfect world every teacher would have his/her own classroom with abundant storage space. But it is not a perfect world, so we have to face the fact that a collection of any kind requires space.

The type of system you create will need to fit in the space that you have available while being readily accessible to you and the students. I have used everything from file folders in a portable cardboard box to pizza boxes that could be stacked on the floor. The artifacts that you will be collecting will have a direct bearing on the size and shape of your containers. But don't let space limitations become a barrier. Where there is a will, there is a way. Be creative.

Although there are only four S's in assessment, there is still another S word that should be mentioned. That is *self*. When we assess students we often stop once we have made the judgments on them. This is unfortunate. Teachers need to take a look at the big picture, the "group" photo. Ask yourself what you can learn about the way you taught from looking at the student artifacts. What worked? What didn't work? What do you need to reteach?

After thinking about the S's of assessment, you should have a clearer idea of the concept and factors involved with assessment portfolios and are ready to move ahead into the specifics of establishing an assessment portfolio system of your own.

3. What Is an Assessment Portfolio?

In its most basic form a portfolio is simply a collection of a student's work that reflects individual growth and progress over a period of time. Few educators, if any, would disagree with the notion that the portfolio is potentially an ideal tool for assessing student learning. The problem then becomes taking the concept to full implementation. This is the point at which many teachers give up and say that it is too large a task or it will increase their workload too much. However, I believe sincerely that if you have honestly looked at your four S's, *students, style, subject,* and *space,* you should be ready to take the next step. The hardest work lies in your forethought and planning, not in the efforts of implementation. I have found that portfolios have cut my paper load dramatically, so I do not spend nearly the time I used to spend grading student work. An unexpected by-product of implementing a portfolio system has been my desire to find new and creative evaluation tools to include in the students' collections. Assessment has become more meaningful, interesting, less judgmental, and almost fun for both my students and myself.

re identifying some specific steps to take in creating class-
ssessment portfolios, I want to share with you the Lustig
of Portfolio Assessment. This model simply represents the
bjectives, the desired outcomes, and the process of insti-
essment portfolios.

In the 1970s when I was living in southern California, many of my friends adopted a trendy philosophy called "EST." I remember that the driving force of this lifestyle was to do what was best for **Them**, the *T* in EST. I thought that this was selfish, and as I grew older I came to realize that doing what is best for **Them** often meant doing what was clearly harmful to others. As a teacher I firmly believe that we must do what is best for the **S**tudents. Hence the shift from "EST" to "ESS." Which brings us to the Lustig Model of Portfolio Assessment. It all centers around doing what is best for the students.

students ass es s
their progr es s
and see succ es s
through acc es s

This model makes it clear that the entire process of portfolio assessment centers around the suffix "ESS." This reflects the concept that we begin assessment portfolios with the end in mind, we plan the "snapshots" that we are going to take of our learners. By utilizing the photos we place into the album, students will be able to ass**ess** their progr**ess** and to see their succ**ess** through having acc**ess** to the portfolio.

With this concept and its goal in mind, we are ready to present the specific elements involved in creating your own portfolio system. The result of your system will be a collection of student work, but we need to discuss some of the construction materials needed to build the final product. We know that even the best plan does not lead to a great structure without the right materials and tools. Your system will need to involve and incorporate five components:

a container, a philosophy, an ongoing process, a variety, and a selection.

First, a portfolio is a container. As mentioned earlier, the choice of a container is limited only by your imagination. The main qualification is that it be able to hold a representative sample of student work. You will need to go back and think of your responses to the analysis of your students, style, subject, and space before you decide on the ideal container for your situation.

In my case a folder works well because I keep a writing portfolio on each student. These folders are kept in a file cabinet that I saved from the trash. I had a custodian drill the lock out since there were no keys, and now my students have complete and unconditional access to their folders. In the beginning I wasn't so fortunate. Without a classroom of my own I traveled from room to room, so I needed a portable system. I still chose to use file folders, but each class's portfolios were kept in a discarded paper box from the copier room. It wasn't attractive, but it was functional. Over time I developed the desire to keep larger items such as video tapes and three-dimensional projects in the collections. This led me to create from cereal boxes supplemental portfolios for each student on my team. This works well and prevents these items from falling out. These cereal box portfolios contain work from all classes, not just language arts.

If space is limited, try using pizza boxes. They stack nicely and provide a lot of room. A kindergarten teacher I worked with was concerned that her student artifacts were too large and bulky to keep an ongoing collection. After a little thought, I suggested that each child bring in a plastic laundry basket to hold his/her "stuff." It worked out very well. Consider what you and the students need. In brainstorming possibilities a good solution will appear.

No matter what kind of container you decide on, make sure to include a form to be completed whenever any item is taken from or added to the collection. This form provides a running record of transactions and should include the date, what the item is, student evaluation or reaction to it, and possibly teacher comments on it. (A sample form is included on page 26.) This record will help jar both student and teacher memories as time goes on.

The portfolio must also reflect a philosophy that embraces the concept of learning as a process, something that is always happening. It should also affirm the idea that assessment and teaching should be closely related. Lastly, your philosophy must recognize the importance of the informal and exploratory work that went into the final product.

Making a shift in philosophy is tough. It was for me. I had to believe in my heart that if students were "doing," they were learning. As teachers we tend to want to correct and give advice each step of the way. I found it hard to step back and put my red pen down. I had to let students learn as they went along and only offer advice and guidance. The result was far more student ownership of their work and a higher level of learning. To help solve the need for entries in the grade book, I developed what I call *work-in-progress* grades. Students can obtain full credit for reaching established checkpoints on due dates. This enables me to monitor the task while encouraging student control of the product. Doing the work for them along the way only teaches them to seek help whenever there is a problem, it doesn't encourage exploration and the use of higher-level thinking skills. It is in the doing that the learning takes place.

Students' portfolios should provide illustrations of an ongoing learning process. Learning is not something that happens one day and then you are done. Likewise an assessment should reflect this ongoing growth. As you plan your lessons and evaluations revisit earlier additions to the portfolios. Create assignments that are similar in nature to earlier ones and that check on previously studied skills. This will give the students and you items to contrast and compare as reflection occurs.

Keep in mind that the portfolio is not the assessment, it is a tool to use in making an assessment of student progress. Too often teachers tend to want to assess the portfolio not the progress the student has made. Our goal, remember, is to ass**ess** student progr**ess** in order that they can see succ**ess** through having acc**ess** to the collection. It is the progression of each individual student that we are seeking to discover; it is the process as much as the product that we want to assess.

That brings us to the component of variety. Your portfolios should include a variety of materials. These various artifacts should represent different points along the way toward developing the final product. If you only include the final products students will not discover the growth achieved and the obstacles that they overcame as they progressed. When students are given time to reflect on their various artifacts accumulated over a period of time, they will recognize the steps they took. Far more learning takes place in getting to the final outcome than is derived from handing in only the end product. As teachers we must demonstrate that concept in our assessment strategies, for if we don't deem it important neither will our students.

The variety of artifacts in the collection should also touch on the diversity of learning modalities and intelligences. If we only evaluate one type of work over and over, the students that are good at that type of task will do well, while other students may never be able to show their true potential. Recently, the truth of this generalization became particularly apparent as I am now on an inclusion team. With the supported education students in my classroom, I have realized that every student has abilities that our "normal" classrooms don't tap. Teaching in most classrooms tends to be an audio, verbal/linguistic method of passing on information. When I provided more visual and kinesthetic options I began to reach and excite many students that had often given up. By including these modalities into your portfolios both the strengths and weaknesses of the students will be reflected.

Lastly, the portfolio needs to include items selected. Both the student and the teacher should be allowed to make choices regarding what is included. I have certain items that I require to be included in their collection, but I encourage students to add things I don't ask for, things that they think are good examples of their progress. Likewise, I periodically let them remove something that they don't want me to see or evaluate. The result over time is that individual portfolios are very different one from another, but they all celebrate the individuality of each child. Having the students involved in the selection process also helps to create an ownership of their portfolios. They are their photo albums not mine.

An assessment portfolio system is many things. It is so much more than a collection of papers in a folder. It is a powerful tool to use in measuring growth and learning over a period of time. It helps the student and the teacher to focus on where the student has been in order to determine where he/she should go next. It is the nearly perfect vehicle by which to ass**ess** student progr**ess** in order to see succ**ess** through having acc**ess** to prior learning. Most importantly it is the best system for the student. 🗀

Portfolios are time machines that take you through your writing process.

4. Establishing a Plan

Whatever plan you are going to put into place must be a system that works for you. It has to be compatible with your **S**tudents, your **S**tyle, your **S**ubject, and available **S**pace. Once you have given each of the four S's careful thought you are ready to establish a more detailed plan of attack. As the next elements in establishing an assessment portfolio system are discussed, continue to remind yourself that this will only work if it is manageable for you. I cannot tell you exactly how to do it; I can only provide a skeleton. How your system builds upon that skeleton is up to you.

The plan that you implement needs to include five essential components: (1) student access, (2) student ownership, (3) relevant items, (4) organization, and (5) sharing. Without these five elements an otherwise well-planned portfolio system will not achieve the desired results. Your plan needs to interlock these five factors into a unique combination that reflects your personality and the needs of students.

First, a look at student access. As mentioned earlier, students must have access to their portfolios. This is essential as the goal is for students to take responsibility for their own assessment. This cannot happen unless the students can compare and contrast their work over a period of time.

There are really two ways to accommodate student access. The first way is for you, the teacher, to provide time for access as a part of your lesson plans. I do this on what I call Portfolio Days. These are scheduled days when students have an entire class period to get their portfolios out and spend time with them. During this time, students can go back in time and begin to see their growth. Of course this may never happen if you tell them this is what they are supposed to do. You can facilitate this, however, through guided objectives which will give their perusing structure and direction. I usually list a series of tasks on the board for them to accomplish during that class period. These might include updating the required "Welcome to My Portfolio" letter kept in the front of the collection. This letter explains several things to anyone going through the materials. It explains the style of organization, the favorite and

---

Directions for Welcome to My Portfolio Letter

Write a letter to the people who will be looking at your portfolio. It will be kept at the front of your collection, and it should give the information that will help a reader understand your work. This letter will become the tour guide when you are not there.

Please be sure that your letter includes the following:
* How have you organized your collection of work?
* What is your favorite thing included in the portfolio; why?
* What is the one thing that you wish wasn't included; why?
* What thing did you work the hardest on, and why was it so hard for you?
* What project came easiest for you; why?
* What concept are you currently focusing on as you continue your work?
* What is at least one realization you have had about your work after you have looked at the collection and reflected on everything that is included?
* Any other information that you think would be helpful to someone looking at your portfolio.

A Student's Letter

10/27/95

Dear Reader,

Welcome to my portfolio. I have organized my portfolio so that language arts is on the right side and math and science are on the left side. My favorite thing in my portfolio is my Carmen San Diego project because I work hard on it and my efforts paid off. I am very satisfied with everything in my portfolio. I don't know what the hardest thing to do in my portfolio is because I did my best on every project. The project that came easiest to me was the learning styles because I enjoyed rating myself and I found out how I learn the best. The concept I am keeping in mind as I continue to work throughout the year is to do the best I can on every project and assignment. After looking at my work I have realized that how much detail I put into it. I hope you enjoy my portfolio.

R.A. (a seventh grader)

least favorite item in the collection, and what is the current focus of their efforts. As the students write or rewrite this letter periodically they are being directed into self-reflection. Other activities during a Portfolio Day might be to reorganize the items in their portfolio or to chose a partner and share something. Both of these activities will be covered in more detail later in this chapter. The activities during this structured time are limited only by your imagination as you seek to create an environment for constructive reflection.

The second type of student access is perhaps the most meaning-ful yet it is the hardest to achieve. This is when students go to their portfolio on their own. They may be adding something, retrieving something, placing something for safekeeping or just for personal reflection. As the facilitator you can only encourage this, you can-not force it. Some students will do this naturally and frequently, while others may never do it on their own. This does not mean your system is a failure. It only means that some students aren't quite ready to take on the full responsibility of self-assessment. You can encourage students to utilize their portfolios on their own by what you include in their collection or by how you suggest they utilize it. For example, I encourage those less organized students to keep any important papers that they will need for other classes in their portfolios. They feel it is a safe place that belongs to them. This concept also promotes ownership, which is the second key component of your plan.

The students must feel ownership in the entire system and in particular of their own portfolios. They must believe they are their collections not yours. There are several ways to create this idea. Probably the easiest and quickest way is to let them decorate their containers to express their individuality. This usually includes draw-ings and collages, but all things are possible. Some students get very creative in their approach to personalizing their containers. I have had students that add another picture on the cover to repre-sent what they are adding each time. Others create a jigsaw puzzle effect and color in another piece each time they add a work. Still others just add on to the designs as the year goes on. These decora-tions not only provide a feeling of ownership, but they can also provide yet another tool to assess growth and changes in the stu-dents. Two years ago I had a very troubled young man, Bryan, in one of my classes. As the year began all of the decor on his portfo-lio was in black and strongly suggested death and violence. By the end of the year this boy had undergone some changes in self-esteem and this was reflected on his portfolio. His drawings were now in color and centered on sports. Both he and I were able to see and discuss the changes at our end of the year portfolio conference. This discussion might not have taken place if he hadn't been able to express himself by decorating his container.

Another way that students can feel ownership of their portfolios is by having some say about what is in the collection. There are always certain things I require to be in the portfolios, but I always encourage them to add things on their own. They can add illustrations, work from other classes, or even extra projects they have completed outside of class. It makes no difference what they add beyond what I require, yet if they want it to be part of the total assessment for my class they must be able to relate it to language arts. It is also important to allow them to be able to remove something from their collection periodically. Even as adults we sometimes do something that we are not particularly proud of. Once the collection in the portfolio begins to grow, it is quite acceptable to let students remove something that they don't want you to see. Remember that we want them to learn to present their best. Making the choice to remove something again forces reflection and evaluation while providing a feeling of ownership. The interesting thing that I have found is that when given the opportunity to remove something, most students choose not to remove anything. It is still a part of them, no matter how much they dislike it. It is simply a poor snapshot that still tells some part of their story and likely has a part in showing progress.

This brings us to relevant items. The works and samples that are kept in the portfolios need to be relevant to what the learners have been doing and how they have been growing. In other words, they need to demonstrate the changes that learning in your class has brought about. To include a math test in my writing portfolio would do little good toward my assessment of the student in writing class. However, a collection of essay tests from other subjects would help assess the student's growth in writing essay answers, a skill I am primarily responsible for teaching.

I strongly suggest that the collection of relevant items include a wide variety of types of work, ones that utilize several learning modalities and intelligences. Although it is important to include varied selections, you must also include several items of the same type, samples from different times during the year. Without similar items there is nothing there to compare or contrast during reflection time.

The items included should demonstrate learning in all three levels of the assessment hierarchy: (1) acquisition of knowledge, (2) application of knowledge, and (3) use of knowledge. They also should include work from the informal exploration done en route to the final project. The collection should include, but is not limited to the following: work samples, homework samples, measures of comprehension such as short answer questions, essays, test and quiz samples, and journaling samples.

Other important items are special notes and periodic observations made by the teacher and student reflections. The teacher observations should be comments that help provide an individualized focus and learning goal for the student. These can be very informal notes, comments on individual works, an ongoing articulation sheet, checklists, and/or conference summaries.

Student reflections can also take many forms. I usually ask for some kind of reflection on each item as it is placed in the portfolio. I also require a written reflection from the student prior to each periodic portfolio conference with me. Since I feel that student reflection loses something when it is forced, much of the reflection my students do is very informal and subtle. The way they organize the items, their letter "Welcome to My Portfolio," and having the opportunity to discard an item are all ways that bring about self-reflection and evaluation of their own work.

As with any collection, there must be some kind of order, and organization is the fourth key component of your plan. Most family photo albums are arranged in chronological order, and this certainly works well in a portfolio system. I, however, do not like to dictate how the students organize their collections. I have found that giving them the freedom of how to organize their portfolios promotes individuality while promoting ownership. Since students are always in a state of change and growth, they sometimes change the organization as often as seventh grade girls change their best friend. Allowing them to choose the organization plan may lead to frequent changes, but each time a change occurs they must do some reflecting Some students choose chronological order while others choose favorite to least favorite, largest to smallest, or even alphabetical. The only criterion is that some kind of logic is present in the organization. I do ask them to explain their organization in the welcoming letter.

I also have a simple organization sheet that each student keeps at the front of his/her collection. This record sheet provides a record of the date of entry, the nature of and title of the item, reflection on it, and my comment should I choose to make one. This log provides an always-current list of items in the order they were added.

Portfolio Entry Log

Quarter	Date	Assignment/Title	Student Comments	Teacher Comments (optional)

It also provides a cross reference checklist for both student and teacher to make sure all required items are included.

While I have given the choice of organization to the student, you may wish to maintain control of how the portfolios are organized, particularly during the system's maiden voyage. I chose the open approach so that students would take primary responsibility for their portfolios. I also admit to having the hidden agenda of decreasing my personal workload.

There are other items that can be incorporated into the portfolio's organization. Such things as checklists of goals or objectives covered can be included. These may be particularly useful in reporting on state or local learning outcomes. I suggest that you incorporate as much as possible of your assessment workload into the portfolio system. The purpose here is not to add another layer of assessment but to incorporate as much as possible into a single, sound, and manageable program.

The last critical component of your plan is sharing. Students need to be given ample opportunity to share their work and their progress. Sharing forces them to formalize and verbalize their thoughts and reflections. This sharing can be with peers, teachers, and/or parents.

When students share with others, usually the most common problem is the excessive use of one of these two assessment statements: "This is the best thing I've ever read; I wouldn't change a thing!" or "This stinks!" The best way to overcome these presumably well meant evaluations is to prepare students to be critical evaluators. This will not only help them to be better peer evaluators but better analysts of their own work. Developing their ability to be good critics takes time and work, but it can be done. In the meantime, I suggest you use a simple three point system. After a sharing session have receivers list three specific things: one thing they liked, one thing they would change, and one question they would ask. This usually will provide a well-balanced initial evaluation. A peer input form of this nature follows.

Peer Reflection/Sharing Input Form

Student providing the input_____

The project belongs to_____

The assignment is _____

Something I liked was _____

Because _____

Something I did not understand was_____

Because _____

A question I would like to ask is _____

Something I would like to know more about is_____

I would like to make these general comments regarding the project's strengths and weaknesses _____

If I were giving this project a grade, I would give it a(n)___

Because _____

When students share their work with the teacher they are somewhat reluctant to speak freely. They have been conditioned to let you tell them what is wrong or right with the work; so put down your red pencil and become a listener. Let the students do the talking; they know much more about their work than we give them credit for. (Additional comments about student-teacher sharing are provided in the chapter on conferencing.)

Students also need to share at least some selections with their parents or a significant other outside of school. Sometimes I send an item home with an evaluation form to be completed by some relative or neighbor. As much as we would like for parents to take an active role in the education of their children, we also know that this isn't always possible, hence the use of an option. The child that can't get a parent to evaluate can use an older sibling, a relative, or a neighbor and not feel left out. I do not send the entire portfolio home at any time; in fact, the portfolios are never allowed out of the classroom. However, I do know of teachers who do let them out for parent evaluation. Again, this is one of those decisions that you will need to make for yourself depending on your students and your style.

Probably the best way to share portfolios with parents is through parent conferences. At conference time I gather a student's writing, team, and advisory portfolios and bring them to the meeting. Artifacts are very powerful tools at any parent-teacher conference or multidisciplinary conference. In student-led conferences the portfolio is the focal point for discussion and goal setting. (This concept is discussed in more detail in the conferencing chapter.)

Although student access, ownership, relevant items, organization, and sharing are not the only components or factors to consider in establishing your portfolio plan, they are the key ones. With the four S's of assessment and the above elements in mind, it is time to begin to put your personal plan on paper. I suggest that you first do a "mini" portfolio, one for a single chapter or unit. This mini unit will enable you to test the waters and find out if your ideas will really work for your subject, students, style, and space. You will also avoid the mistake I made when I started using portfolios. I began by creating year-long portfolios for 150 students. I was well into the project before I realized that some of my ideas just weren't going to work as I thought they would. But it was too late to turn back and start over; I had to live with what I had created for the remainder of the year.

PLANNING MY MINI PORTFOLIO UNIT

1. Briefly describe: your students; your subject; your style; your space;

2. Establishing the plan:
    Subject/chapter/or unit;
    Type of container;
    Location for student access;
    When and how will access occur?
    How will ownership be achieved?
    How will it be organized?
    With whom and how will students share?

    It will include:

1.	6.
2 .	7.
3.	8.
4.	9.
5.	10.

3. Introducing Portfolios:

    To students: When? How?

    To parents:

    To peers:

4. How do you plan to evaluate the portfolios?

5. How will you encourage student reflection?

6. How will you conference with students?

7. In the space below make notes as your unit progresses about things that work and things you would like to change. Also include ideas you would like to try and ideas for other alternative assessments.

At this point complete an initial plan using the planning guide, remembering that it is only a planning sheet and you can change anything as you go. Remember also that this is to be a "mini" unit, a trial at portfolio assessment. Expect to make mistakes, and be ready to make changes in your next plan.

Once you have completed the initial plan (and finished reading this handbook) it is time to give it a go. Try your mini unit to experience the concept firsthand. Then reflect on what you have done. Carefully evaluate the system you set up and make needed changes before doing another unit or launching a full scale portfolio system in your classroom. An important source of data in evaluating your system is student feedback. Find out what they thought, what they learned, and how they think the system could be improved.

Following all that, you are ready to develop a more comprehensive and ongoing plan. You can use the same planning guide for your next try. It is always best to have your plans in black and white before you begin. Good luck. 🗁

Views of a Seventh Grade Teacher

In my class, students keep their reading assignments in a folder. At midterm they reflect on the progress they have made on the goals for the quarter. At the end of the quarter students look over the work in their portfolios.and figure out their grade. Along with a letter I have written to their parents, they are asked to analyze specific strengths and weaknesses in the areas of homework, tests, and projects. From these weaknesses they set two goals. The student signs it, the parents sign it after they have looked over their child's work. I feel portfolios have aided in the maturation and self-knowledge of my students and have helped parents, teachers, and students become partners in learning.

5. Introducing Portfolios

Now that you have thought about and organized a tentative plan, it is time to consider introducing the concept of assessment portfolios to those that will be affected by this system of evaluation. This may sound like an easy job, and it is, but you should realize that this could very well be the single most important step of your portfolio program. You need to provide the specifics of your system carefully while generating the excitement needed to support it and keep the momentum going during the months ahead. You have created a good assessment program, now you must sell it.

There are three groups, all potential advocates, but initially all may be adversaries. These people in the beginning will very likely give you some skeptical looks; but in the end they will wonder why all educators don't use this system. Their questions and doubts will force you to be careful and calculated as you begin assessment portfolios; their comments and support will encourage and fortify you during implementation. As you introduce your portfolio plan, then, you must face head-on these three groups – the students, their parents, and your colleagues.

In introducing your assessment portfolio system my main piece of advice is simple – be honest and open. If you have carefully planned your program, you have nothing to fear. You don't have all the answers, you probably never will, but if you have thought this all out you can't help but communicate the notion that this is indeed best for the students. This form of assessment will help to ensure a good, solid education, and its benefits will shine through as you implement this new concept after introducing it to these three groups. If you are forthright about your intentions and open about your plans, even the most doubting people will at least give you an opportunity to prove yourself.

Before introducing your plan I strongly suggest that you discuss your proposal with your building administrator, if you haven't already. I have never met a supervisor or an administrator that didn't want to be kept informed about what was going on in the building. You must have his/her support and confidence from the very beginning. Almost all principals are open to educational reforms that will benefit learners. Chances are you will be given the green light. If you don't get it, it is quite possible that the plan needs some revision. The buck does stop at the principal's desk, and this is one person you want to be informed fully and in your corner.

Once you have the plan and the go ahead from administration, it is time to introduce this system to the students. Your introduction will set the tone for the entire process, so plan it carefully. Your enthusiasm will be contagious, so don't hold back. If you are excited about the prospects of portfolio assessment, your students will share in your optimism. Remember, the entire project will never work without the students buying into it.

Start off by explaining the concept of a portfolio to the class. Why do artists keep one? How does an artist use it? Once students realize that the portfolio is a collection of a person's best and selected works that is used to assess their progress and their potential, they are ready to hear more about establishing a portfolio of their own.

Tell students about the plan you have devised for their classroom. Explain to them what will be placed in the collection, how and when they will have access to it, how they will claim ownership, and how it will promote sharing. You will need to provide students with information on the way you will be assessing the materials in the portfolio and how the informal work along with the formal outcomes will be stressed. The students will begin to grasp the concept that the pressure on them to achieve specific outcomes is actually lightened because you, the teacher, realize that getting there is just as important as the final product. This is something students seem to know but teachers tend to forget.

After going over the specifics, I return to the students the first set of papers that will go into the portfolio. Timing is important. I return the artifacts that will become the first item in their albums and pass out the entry index form to be kept in the front. We fill out this form as a class. I stress that they need to put honest self-reflective feedback in the section for student comments. I have purposely kept my grading comments to a minimum on these papers to illustrate that their reflections are going to become as important as mine. They will no longer wait for me to "give" them a grade. They will now learn to reflect on their own progress and work to "earn" satisfaction by sincere effort.

Now comes the hook. I hand out folders and ask them to get out markers and colored pencils. It is time to start making their portfolios a reflection of who they are. I show them several examples of personalized portfolios from previous years and describe some of the more creative ones that I have seen. Then I let them go. They have the rest of the class period to begin creating a container that expresses their personality. Students never get this done in what remains of that period, so they look forward to the next time we will go into the portfolios. This task in itself does as much for building enthusiasm for portfolio days as anything else.

Now that the students know about your assessment program, the word is out. What a teacher has done is often a primary family dinner topic. The time is ripe to let parents know about this valuable approach to evaluating their son or daughter. Once again, timing is everything. I usually try to introduce portfolios a few days before the fall open house. This promotes parent curiosity and interest in your teaching and assessment techniques. A large part of my time with parents centers around the use of portfolios. This provides a perfect opportunity for me to stress how much I care about individualized assessment and how anxious I am to incorporate more advanced educational techniques. I tell them about portfolios, something they have never heard of before and something that in almost all cases will improve achievement.

I also discovered that parents dislike red pencil mentality as much as I do. Generally they are tired of their child's becoming discouraged by red marks all over a paper that their child has worked hard to produce. What I call the baseball analogy seems to bring portfolio assessment home. They know that they do not go to a baseball game with the expectation of seeing even the greatest of baseball players hit a home run each time at bat. Likewise, they understand it is unrealistic to expect students to hit a home run each time they complete a project or take a test. It is the overall batting average that counts along with progressive improvement; one time at bat doesn't give an accurate picture of any player's capability.

I follow up open house with a letter to all the parents. This letter explains the concept of assessment portfolios and details the specifics of the plan. I also make frequent references to the system in our quarterly team newsletter. These contacts combined with using the portfolios in conferences and having them participate in some of the reflections throughout the year provide a clear and ongoing picture of how assessment portfolios are being utilized in my classroom.

A Letter to Parents

Dear Parents:

I am writing you this letter to introduce the concept of assessment portfolios and how they will be used in my classroom this year. This is not a radical new way of grading your son or daughter; it is actually an enhancement of how students have traditionally been evaluated. This system will allow you and me, as well as your child, to see his/her progress as the year moves forward.

Each student in my class will create a portfolio that is an organized collection of his/her work over time. It will provide us with items that we can reflect on as they grow throughout the year. This collection will include not only the final projects and tests, it will also include materials that indicate how they got to that end. Another important element in the portfolio will be reflections and self-evaluations. In toto, it will become something like a photo album that shows how they have grown as learners.

I will not be grading every assignment that students complete this year. Students make most of their mistakes during the process of mastering material, so it isn't appropriate to evaluate all items during this period of experimentation. I firmly believe that they are learning as long as they are engaged and doing something, which means that many of the grades I will record are what I refer to as "work in progress" grades. Full credit will be given for completing assignments to the best of their ability and on schedule. Putting red marks on their work as they progress all too often discourages their efforts and willingness to take a risk. We don't expect even the best baseball player to hit a home run each time at bat; and likewise, I don't expect students to produce an "A" project with each assignment. Students will often have a major part in determining their final grade.

Periodically throughout the year, I will have an individual conference with each student about the collection of items in his/her portfolio. We will reflect on the progress that has been made and set goals for future focus. This allows me to individualize my teaching to fit the needs of each unique learner. The portfolio will also be shared with you at parent/teacher conferences or any other time that you would like to make an appointment to see it.

If you have any questions about this system of assessment, please feel free to contact me.

Sincerely

Keith Lustig

The third group to introduce portfolios to is one's colleagues. These are the people that will provide a sounding board for your ideas and revisions as your system grows and expands. Let your peers know what you are doing and how the program is working. In these discourses others will be encouraged to try this approach to evaluation. As more teachers in your building use portfolios, the more sharing and helpful exchanging of ideas occurs. It also provides the grassroots foundation for more sweeping changes in assessment throughout all the schools in your area.

In summary, you need to plan not only your portfolio system, but also how and when you are going to introduce this form of assessment to students, parents, and colleagues. Just as the concept of portfolio assessment is based on creating a collection of artifacts to illustrate growth and progress, so the introduction of the system hinges on a collection of people who will provide support and enthusiasm for the project. This collection of advocates is almost as important as the collections inside the containers. 📁

Reactions from a Reading Teacher

When my pull-out program for at-risk readers changed to a "push-in" program where services were delivered within the regular reading class, I realized that I had a perfect opportunity to begin using a portfolio method of assessing student progress in reading. I wanted to measure the students' attainment of literacy skills in an ongoing and continuous way using the materials that they were actually being asked to read and the writing that they were asked to do.

At first, I was intimidated by the task of organizing a portfolio. At the time it didn't occur to me to start such an assessment with just one unit, using documents and artifacts from a short period of time. At Keith's suggestion, I tried this and was converted. To plan an ongoing assessment, I first of all defined what skilled reading is. Then I decided what things the students were doing that would show evidence that they were progressing toward becoming skilled readers. These are the items that are included in the portfolio. The best part has been watching how adept and intuitive the students have become at assessing themselves.

6. Evaluating Portfolios

Of all of the chapters in this handbook, this one on evaluating portfolios has been the most difficult for me to put down on paper. This is partially true because of my belief that a teacher's evaluation system is as personal as his/her teaching style. There will always be some accepted evaluation guidelines set forth by the state, the district, and sound professional ethics, but educators must exercise flexibility when evaluating students. Just as your portfolio system must reflect your students, subject, and style, so must your evaluation techniques.

To begin with I want to stress the importance of the main purposes of a system of this nature. Keep in mind that a major goal of portfolio assessment is to provide a picture of progress over an extended period of time. Your evaluation design needs to include ways of assessing the attainment of learning goals and objectives that have been set by both student and teacher. You also need to remember that a primary aim of this system of assessment is to guide the student in self-evaluation. The more you involve the learner in the evaluation process the better. Students must become directly responsible for at least a portion of the final evaluation. They should not only take part in developing the assessment process, but also feel they have input and power in its application. This type of involvement will break down the concept that teachers "give" grades.

While deciding on a plan to evaluate your students, keep an open mind and realize that you will have to change your methods of gathering grade book data. This involves focusing on some ideas that may have taken a back seat due to traditions and old habits. As teachers, we often record information in our grade books that was gathered in an easy or quick fashion such as a quiz score but which does not necessarily reflect our learners' growth. Schools have changed, so instruction and assessment procedures should be keeping pace. Will this paradigm shift be a little more difficult and take a little more time? Yes, in the beginning it will, but as time goes on you will find that evaluation will take less time and energy because you will be sharing the responsibility with the student.

As mentioned earlier, the hardest shift for me was to stop and remember that if students are engaged, they are learning. I have always held that belief, but as the years slipped by I had pushed this thought farther and farther to the back of my assessment tool box. This happened because of the almighty need to place numbers or grades in my grade book. Teachers must be accountable; so over time, I focused on more and more end products, grade book entries to show how much I was teaching. These grades may have reflected the outcomes, the formal learning, but did not reflect the ongoing process of growth, the informal progress where learning takes place. Measuring outcomes is always an easier way to evaluate learners because it is presumably so objective and safe. Once you come to recognize that learning is a process not an outcome, you can begin to appreciate a portfolio assessment system.

The collection inside a learner's portfolio reflects the process of growth as well as the formal outcomes. As a student's collection fills you can see that you have far more solid and conclusive data on that child than any collection of number or letter grades in a book could ever provide. Even though you will still close out your grade records at the end of each quarter or semester, a student's portfolio remains open for the year. The ongoing reflection that the portfolio encourages is far more enlightening than a final grade. Long range learning objectives are not achieved in a single six or nine week grading period.

An example is appropriate at this time. Earlier I spoke of Bryan, the student that showed dramatic changes over time with the drawings on the outside of his portfolio. When Bryan came to my class as a sixth grader he was well behind his peers as a writer. His grammar and mechanics were so poor that as a teacher I could not get to the content of his work. If I had been grading Bryan with a traditional English teacher's mind-set, neither Bryan nor I would ever have seen his remarkable progress over the coming months. Even at the end of the year if I had been grading Bryan on each particular product, he would have continued to fail by established standards. The repeated failing grades would have only perpetuated his downward spiral and contributed to his sense of inadequacy. Bryan is a perfect example of a student that was unmotivated and beaten down by grades. Once he was able to see progress in his work over a period of time, he began to believe that he could improve and experience personal successes. By conferencing with Bryan using his portfolio, I was able to help him see the significant growth he had made.

With a portfolio system you are able to factor into the total evaluation that important element of progress. It should not be the only factor in arriving at the final grade, but it should be a part of it. Was Bryan, for example, an "A" student? No, far from it, but he certainly wasn't a failure either. By looking at the entire photo album of a student the teacher is able to assess the whole child.

When establishing an evaluation system that incorporates portfolio assessment, you need to consider the assessment hierarchy discussed in Chapter 1. Assessment works on several levels; that is one of the things that distinguishes it from grading. The portfolio is not the assessment, it is a tool to use in reaching the final assessment. It should contain a collection of artifacts representing all three levels of the hierarchy.

First, the collection needs to contain items that reflect the acquisition of knowledge. Tests, quizzes, and objective worksheets will reflect a student's achievement of knowledge objectives. These items are an important element of the total evaluation, and I record these grades into my grade book at the time I evaluate them. Selected artifacts from this level of the hierarchy are kept in the portfolio as bench marks and for goal setting during student-teacher conferences.

Once the knowledge is acquired, it should be applied. Items that reflect the application of knowledge, the next level of the hierarchy, will comprise the bulk of the contents in the student's collection. Homework assignments, work in progress notes, writing samples, checklists, and projects of various kinds will reveal application. A great deal of this work should be the informal process indicators discussed earlier. Make sure that examples of all phases of the work are collected and kept. Such items will indicate to both student and teacher the ongoing course of learning that is taking place.

It is at this level that students should be encouraged to take risks and experiment. These may be items that students can periodically weed out without fear that mistakes will be held against them. The real problem for the teacher comes to play at this level of evaluation. It is not easy to evaluate how learners use the information they have acquired.

This is where the belief that if students are actively engaged they are learning becomes so important. I have solved the dilemma of how to keep grades in the book at this level by creating what I call work-in-progress grades. I set deadlines and expectations for the various steps along the way, mini outcomes of achievement. Each step takes on a point value in my grade book that is proportionate to the outcome of the total objective and the final grade for the term. The points the students earn are based on their meeting the time line set forth and the effort they put into meeting that mini objective. This enables me to individualize my expectations for students based on their abilities and personal needs. This system allows me to record points for the process as well as the final product. It sends a clear message to the learners that how they do the job is directly related to and is as important as the product itself, perhaps even more important.

The last level of the hierarchy, using the knowledge, is reflected through evaluation of the entire portfolio and the students' reflections on their work. These two elements directly indicate how the learners will use the knowledge to their benefit. The actual portfolio shows clearly how students manage the content of their learning. How students organize, record, and maintain the contents indicates how much and what they value about the knowledge and skills gained. The students' reflections on individual items and their "Welcome to My Portfolio" letters clearly reflect their ability to set priorities and goals regarding the learning process. The reflections also provide a clear indication of how this information will be transferred to other learning situations.

When placing a final evaluation on the portfolio there are various outcomes that you can consider. As always, it is important to explain these expectations to students when establishing a portfolio system. I suggest the use of a rubric or student checklist. Factors that deserve consideration include: completion and inclusion of all required artifacts, meeting all due dates, completed entry log, neatness, organization, participation in peer evaluations, participation in conferences, use of portfolio work time, and personal reflections. A possible set of criteria that might be used for grading portfolios follows.

The grade you place on the portfolio itself needs to be proportionate to the other grades you have collected for the other two levels of the assessment hierarchy. I cannot tell you how much value to assign to each element in this process because it will vary from teacher to teacher and from subject to subject, as it should. I

Criteria for Grading Portfolios

To get an "A" you must:
- Complete and include all assignments that are to be in your portfolio on time
- Completely and accurately fill in your log of entries
- Actively and cooperatively participate in peer reviews and sharing
- Utilize class time designated for portfolio work
- Show evidence of setting and working toward personal goals
- Put time and thought into your personal reflections
- Maintain a neat and organized portfolio
- Actively participate in portfolio conferences

To get a "B" you must:
- Complete and include all assignments that are to be in your portfolio
- Completely and accurately fill in your log of entries
- Actively participate in peer reviews and sharing
- Utilize class time designated for portfolio work
- Show evidence of setting and working toward personal goals
- Put time and thought into your personal reflections
- Maintain an organized portfolio
- Participate in portfolio conferences

To get a "C" you must:
- Complete and include most assignments that are to be in your portfolio
- Completely fill in your log of entries
- Participate in peer reviews and sharing
- Utilize most of the class time designated for portfolio work
- Show evidence of trying to set and work toward personal goals
- Complete personal reflections
- Maintain an organized portfolio
- Participate in portfolio conferences

To get a "D" you must:
- Complete and include some assignments that are to be in your portfolio
- Occasionally fill in your log of entries
- Occasionally participate in peer reviews and sharing
- Utilize some of the class time designated for portfolio work
- Show evidence of setting some personal goals
- Complete a few personal reflections
- Maintain a moderately organized portfolio
- Attend portfolio conferences

To get an "F" you would:
- Complete and include a few of the assignments that are to be in your portfolio
- Seldom fill in your log of entries

personally place the greatest value on the application of knowledge level. I assign approximately twenty percent of the quarter's total points to the acquisition level, sixty percent to the application level, and twenty percent to the use of knowledge level. These percentages are not etched in stone, and they change from quarter to quarter depending on what I am teaching at the time. Remember, it all has to fit your students, subject, and style.

No matter how you decide to evaluate your students and their portfolios, keep in mind that the informal work is equally, if not more important than the formal work. Be sure your evaluation encourages and rewards risk-taking and consistent work toward personal goals. The various elements leading to the overall evaluation should include tests, quizzes, observations, work in progress samples, and student reflections. This collection of "photographs" will combine to fill the pages of the albums.

The driving forces of assessment portfolio evaluation should always relate back to the overall objectives of the concept. Your evaluations need to provide means of identifying individual student strengths, weaknesses, and progress. This is the turning point in getting students involved and interested in developing their own self-evaluation skills. A form that involves both student and teacher assessments of work habits can be found on the next page.

The last step when evaluating portfolios is to evaluate the system itself. If you remember, one of the reasons for assessment is for teachers to evaluate what they have done. This evaluation will provide the needed feedback to decide if students are ready to move on and if you have achieved the curriculum objectives; it will help you decide what, if anything, needs to be revisited. As educators we find ourselves so very busy that often we don't take this final step in the evaluation process. Teacher self-evaluation should take place during the year as well as at the end of it.

I have found that one easy and worthwhile way to complete this final step is to simply ask the students. I provide them with a series of guided questions at the end of a unit or the end of the year that will provide me with their impressions of this method of as-

Name _____ Date _____

STUDENT SELF-ASSESSMENT

	never	seldom	usually	often	always
	1	2	3	4	5
Utilizes work time					
Prepared for class (book, binder, homework)					
Completes assignments on time					
Homework completed thoroughly					
Participates in class					
Seeks help when needed					
Arrives on time					
Exhibits good organization skills					
Work displays care and effort					

TEACHER ASSESSMENT

	never	seldom	usually	often	always
	1	2	3	4	5
Utilizes work time					
Prepared for class (book, binder, homework)					
Completes assignments on time					
Homework completed thoroughly					
Participates in class					
Seeks help when needed					
Arrives on time					
Exhibits good organization skills					
Work displays care and effort					

sessment as well as other aspects of my teaching. By using student feedback and my ongoing personal observations and reflections of the system, I am able to revise and enhance my assessment portfolio system each year. 🗁

7. Conferencing

The last major component of your portfolio system is the matter of conferencing. This is a critical element in establishing a successful plan. Through personal portfolio conferences with students and perhaps parents, you will be able to guide your learners in setting individual goals and engaging in meaningful self-assessment.

Although this may sound like one of the easiest tasks in implementing a system of this nature, it actually can be one of the most difficult. The first concern is making the conferences meaningful and productive. It takes careful planning and forethought to create the proper tone to lead learners to productive realizations. The second obstacle is changing your personal mind-set from that red pencil mentality to being a listener and mentor. Lastly, and very critical, is planning activities for the rest of your students to do while you have one-on-one conferences. If the other students are not on task while you conference, you will be distracted and interrupted repeatedly.

In this chapter I will discuss both teacher-student conferences and teacher-parent-student conferences. Holding conferences between teacher and student is critical to the concept of portfolio assessment. These should be held as frequently as possible, but a bare minimum would be twice a year. The conferences that involve the parents are an incredibly powerful tool, but they are not essential to the success of your program.

As mentioned, there are three important aspects to consider when holding these meetings: careful planning to ensure the intended purpose is achieved, having the correct mind-set as a teacher going into the conference, and keeping the other students actively engaged so you can confer without interruption. If you can conquer these three obstacles, your conferences will not only benefit your learners, they will also become highlights of your job.

Careful planning for the conferences not only relieves fear and stress for both the teacher and the student, it will also ensure that the meeting has structure and will meet the needs of both parties involved. The structure that you provide should encourage reflection prior to the actual encounter. This reflection will help narrow the focus of the conference so the most meaningful information is shared and the meeting adheres to the time limit set.

The best way to gain the needed structure is to inform the students of exactly what to expect and to reinforce the fact that you will be talking "with" them not "at" them. My first suggestion is to prepare a video tape of a simulated conference. Have a colleague play the role of a student and show the class exactly what will be happening when they meet with you. This will not only put the students at ease about what to expect, it will also model the behavior and amount of student participation that you are seeking.

Once the class has seen the video and asked questions about what to expect, have the students prepare some kind of written reflection so they have a focus before they sit down with you. Depending on my focus for the conference, I have used two different techniques to achieve this. One way is to provide them with a series of questions to be answered about their portfolio collection. These questions should center around the information that you want to obtain at that point in the evaluation process. You definitely want them to include their reflections on their strengths, weaknesses, progress, and future focus for improvement. You can ask them what they feel is their best work and why, their worst and why, the problems they have encountered, or how they felt when they completed a particular work. No matter what you ask the students to reflect on, always be sure that they include a personal goal for their future work.

Conference Preparation Questions

Please answer the following questions about your portfolio collection and bring the answers with you to our conference.

1. Explain how you have your portfolio organized and why you chose to keep it in this order.
2. What thing in your portfolio are you most proud of? Why?
3. What item would you most like to remove from this collection? Why?
4. Off all the assignments included here, which one was the hardest for you? Why?
5. Which assignment would you most like to redo? Why?
6. What have you been working on this year to improve? Has it improved? Why or why not?
7. What general areas do you think that you need to work on to improve your future work? Why?
8. What is the one thing that you would want someone to notice about your portfolio? Why?
9. Do you feel that this collection of work really reflects your abilities and what you have achieved this year? Why or why not?
10. If you could change anything about this portfolio system what would it be? Why?

We will complete the following statement at the conference together. My specific goal to work on before the next conference is.....

Another way to provide focus for conferences is to have students evaluate a piece of their own work using the same assessment tool that I will use. I have the students select one item that they want me to evaluate for a major grade, their "home run" artifact. I provide them with the actual tool that I will use when I assess the piece. Oftentimes I have the class help me create this tool. This process provides the opportunity for them to have direct input into what is being evaluated, thus providing the very important element of ownership. The students then evaluate their selection with the tool we have created which uses a holistic 1-5 rating system for each objective. They put S for student, indicating how they would assess their work for each item. I then collect the papers and assess them, placing a T for teacher that I believe is appropriate for each item. I have found over time that 95% of what the students decide on in this process is exactly how I would have assessed the piece.

When we sit down for our conference, we focus our discussion on the items where there is a difference in our view of the work, not the ones on which we agree. During the discussion the student has an opportunity to explain any rating that is different from mine. If the reasoning is valid, and it often is, I move my rating to something we agree upon. When we have completed the evaluation we total the T's, and that total becomes the grade. With this technique the students not only help create the evaluation/conference instrument, they also are actively involved in the final grade placed on their work and have an understanding of how that grade was assigned. Lastly, as with any conference, we set a goal to work on and write it down in the portfolio so it is highly visible.

No matter how much you plan to ensure a clear focus for your conferences, they will not be successful if you don't go into the meeting with the proper frame of mind. Remember that the time for instruction has passed; this is the time for evaluation. You need

Student/Teacher Evaluation of a Paper

Please rate yourself 1 (poor) to 5 (excellent) on each of the
following items by putting an "S" in the box that reflects your
opinion of your work. I will place a "T" where I would
evaluate each item before we conference on this piece.

	0	1	2	3	4	5	Comments
Mechanics							
Punctuation							
Capitalization							
Spelling							
Verb usage							
Sentence sense							
Structure							
Paragraphing							
Introduction							
Body							
Conclusion							

	0	1	2	3	4	5	Comments
Content							
Vocabulary							
Focus							
Mood							
Creativity							
Originality							
Misc.							
Planning							
Neatness							
Characters							
Interest							
Style							
Effort							

General comments: TOTAL :   /100 literally to put the red pencil down. This is hard for a teacher to do, but it is critical for the success of the conference. At first I couldn't talk to a student without that pen or pencil in my hand, so I actually had to sit on my hands until I got used to the idea. Your job now is to listen not tell. Listen to how you can help; the students will tell you if you only give them the opportunity. At first this is awkward for both of you, but as time goes on it becomes easier. When you do speak, don't point out the problems and the errors, let them do that. They will be their own worst critic and will take the criticism far better since they are giving it rather than you. It is your role to point out what you like, ask questions about things that are confusing, and make that all-important suggestion for a future focus. If you can stick to this type of input, the conference will remain positive and therefore productive.

Ralph Fletcher (1992) recommends six rules for teachers when conferencing with students:

1. Keep the conference short, five to seven minutes.
2. Don't use a pencil while conferencing.
3. Let the student respond first, how does he/she see the work? Let the student spot the problems.
4. Respond to content not form.
5. Remember that the student can reject suggestions.
6. Focus on teaching the student not the material, your job is more to improve the learner than the work.

Now you are ready to hold your conferences, but are the students ready to let you? The last important factor to consider is how to keep the other students occupied with meaningful tasks while you hold your meetings. What you have them do during this time will greatly depend on your "S's" (students, subject, and style). I have found that a high-interest project works far better than busy work such as worksheets or book exercises. An ace in your pocket

is the fact that your students will be excited about these conferences. The idea of having your total attention for a period of time
is more meaningful to them than you can imagine. Openly remind
them that in order for these conferences to take place you will
need cooperation from everyone, not just from the student in the
conference. The meeting that may be interrupted or cut short could
very well be theirs if the entire class doesn't unite in its effort to
stay on task. Such activities as a guided novel study, a creative
writing project, illustrating a story or even portfolio review time all
work well to productively occupy the class while you conference.
This is not a time for cooperative group work as, by its nature, it
can be distracting.

After the conference, students should reflect on the meeting and
process what was discussed, using a form such as the one shown
here.

Conference Reflections

Before our conference I was worried about:

I was anxious to share:

During the conference I felt:

I really liked it when:

The best thing the teacher told me was:

After the conference I felt:

The biggest thing I learned was:

The next time I have a conference I will:

Another type of portfolio conferencing involves the parents of
the student. In this model the students are responsible for leading
the parent-teacher conference using their portfolio as a tool to show

their progress and growth. If a parent is not available, the student should be provided with some significant other from their life or from within the school staff. The ground rules already discussed still hold true, but the planning takes on a different focus. Since the student is leading the conference it is helpful to provide a script or format to follow. It is also important to provide a rehearsal for the student prior to the actual conference with the parent.

SAMPLE SCRIPT

What do I say to my parents at my conference?

"Thank you for coming to my conference. I have 30 minutes to present to you my portfolio. When we are done with the conference, we will be setting some citizenship and academic goals together."

"Mom and Dad, do you have any questions yet?"

"This is my student-led conference folder. (Open it and turn it so your parents can read it.) Here I have the "Welcome to My Portfolio" letter, a letter you wrote to me, a graph of my grades, my progress report and report cards, my first quarter goal sheets, a study habits checklist, examples of my work, a friendship form, and any disciplinary actions."

"When we are done looking at these items, together we will complete three forms. These will include setting academic goals, reflecting on our conference, and evaluating our conference."

Read these letters and forms aloud to your parents. You don't have to read the letter they wrote you. Just thank them for it! Let them read along as you read aloud. They may have comments or questions as you move from paper to paper. Stop and do your best to answer them if they do.

"Well, now it's time to look at the graph of my grades, my progress report, and my report card along with examples of my work and a study habits evaluation form. Which class do you want to see first?" (Wait for them to answer.)

Make sure you locate and present each progress report and graph immediately. Give them a few minutes to examine these before you flip through the other papers in the folder. Let your parents turn the pages of your work if they want to. Answer any questions they may have. Straighten papers after everyone has seen them and put them back in the folder. Keep the progress report and graph out if your parents want to hold on to them. Perhaps you can place them in your student-led conference folder for later reference.

Conferences of this nature do take longer to complete, but the benefits are many. The student becomes directly responsible to the parent for his/her learning and progress. The nature of this system requires that student reflection must go very deep in order to process the information to be shared, draw conclusions about the work, and be able to answer the questions that will be raised.

Another positive aspect from the teacher's point of view is the fact that more than one conference can be held at a time. If the students are properly prepared, the teacher can float from conference to conference providing comments, support, and guidance.

One of the eighth grade teams at Hill has been conducting student-led conferences for three years with great success. The team modeled its system on a plan presented at the NMSA conference in Portland, Oregon. The ideas, put forth by Lynn Lee Lacey of Larsen Bay, Alaska, provided the team with ample food for thought and sample forms to start them in the right direction. Sarah Leudke, the team leader at Hill, says, "I have never seen such meaningful conferences. I can't imagine doing it any other way. The portfolios provide the student accountability needed to make the learning strategies set at the conference successful."

A letter that explains student-led conferences follows along with an actual conference reflection prepared by a student and an evaluation form prepared by a parent.

Team Letter Explaining Student-Led Portfolio Conferences

Dear Parents/Guardians of Team 7-2

Our first parent conferences will be held on November 9th and 10th.

This fall, Team 7-2 students will conduct their conferences by presenting portfolios to their parents or guardians. They will show academic work from first quarter, share various self-assessments of personal strengths and weaknesses in their lives as students, and, with our help, will set goals for improvement in 2nd quarter. They will also explain their report card grades.

The team of teachers will quietly monitor the student-parent conferences from the side and are willing to help facilitate if necessary, but your son or daughter will be in charge!

We will be preparing all students for the responsibility of presenting their first quarter work during this special 20 minute conference. Certain projects must be completed, papers must be organized, students must assess themselves in different ways, the portfolios must be created, and students must practice conducting their conferences.

Since you are a central figure in your child's success in school, we ask you to write a letter to your child that will be included in his/her portfolio. Tell how you view him/her as a person, a learner, and a friend. Tell what goals you have for your child. Mention the things that you feel he/she is very good at doing and the things you think need work. Use as many paragraphs as you need to convey to your child your thoughts and feelings about these topics. Share your letter with your child and sent it to school by Wednesday, November 1, 1995.

Teachers who have requested these letters tell us that students are very proud to include them in their portfolios. Thank you for your participation.

We feel these conferences are an important form of self-assessment, and we will be making arrangements for all students to present their portfolios to an adult from Hill if someone from home is not available.

We are very excited about this opportunity for your child, for you, and for us! The student-led conference folders are an excellent tool for promoting responsibility and empowering young people. We are looking forward to seeing you.

Thank you,   Team 7-2 Teachers

Conference Reflections

1. Before my conference I felt *a little nervous but was mostly okay because I'm used to talking to my parents.*
2. Now that my conference is over I feel *good. I liked being there because you know what your parents and teachers are talking about otherwise it's like talking behind your back.*
3. The best part of my conference was *being able to give my own opinion.*
4. I think my parents felt *really good because I was giving the conference.*
5. The next time I conduct a conference with my parents I will *explain the papers more. Some of them were hard to understand.*

Conference Evaluation Listener Form

1. Before the conference, I felt *anxious to see Amanda's work papers and her evaluation.*
2. Now that the conference is over, I feel *it was a good idea to make Amanda "responsible." It's also good practice for speaking skills.*
3. The best part of the conference was *Amanda's excellent report cards and discussion of areas that she needs to work on.*
4. I think my "student" felt *proud of her grades and accomplishments, a little uncomfortable at first but did a fine job.*
5. My suggestions for conferences in the future are *A very good idea — thought the mix of student "learning" with input from the teachers worked very well.*

Setting Academic Goals During Conferences

NAME _____

QUARTER ① 2 3 4

Rate your personal work/study habits and citizenship with *4* reflecting a strength and *1* room for improvement:

WORK AND STUDY HABITS	1	2	3	4	CITIZENSHIP	1	2	3	4
Completes assignments on tims				x	Shows a positive attitude				x
Takes pride in work				x	Respects authority				x
Follows written and oral directions				x	Cooperates with others			x	
Participates in class discussions				x	Follows school rules				x
Shows initiative/ self-direction				x	Shows responsibility for self				x
Does work neatly			x		Shows respect for school property				x
Is well organized			x		Is well groomed				x
Has good listening habits			x		Prompt and regular attendance				x

With input from your parents/guardians and advisor, choose one goal for the next quarter that you feel will improve your work/study habits and one that will improve your citizenship.

Complete these blanks during your conference or shortly thereafter. Ask your advisor for a copy of your goals since he/she will keep the original in your advisory file.

Goal-Setting Form

NAME _____ DATE _____

Long term goal: *make new friends*
By when:
School short-term goal: *Be more open with people*
By when: *By the end of each class I will have talked to one new person*
Things to do: *Talk to people and introduce myself.*

Home short-term goal: *Meet people who live by me*
By when: *when ever kids are outside*
Things to do: *If some kids are playing a game ask if I can play.*

Support I need _____

From _____

By when _____

Evaluation _____

By when _____

Partner/coach _____

I have been making new friends with people at school and out of school. I have also been more open with people. My goals have been achieved but I will still pursue them.

Work and Study Habits

My goal will be *to do more recreational reading*

I need to work on this goal because *I would like to learn more things about the world.*

To accomplish this goal I can *read the newspaper and NewsWeek.*

By the end of the quarter I will know if I have accomplished this goal by *My knowledge of current events.*

> ### Citizenship
> My goal will be *more mannerly*.
>
> I need to work on this goal because *I sometimes forget my manners*
>
> To accomplish this goal I can *always remember my manners*.
>
> By the end of the quarter I will know if I have accomplished by goal by *feed back from my mother*.

Despite the obstacles involved in whatever type of conferences you choose to implement, the rewards for both the students and you are great. It is through these meetings that you can involve the learners directly in their education and personal goal setting. You are able to let each student know that he/she is an individual and has unique strengths and needs. Perhaps most importantly, you are empowering students to take responsibility for their own educational future and to establish specific goals in both the academic and personal/social realms. 🗁

Eighth Graders Assess Portfolios

I think that portfolios are great. They are a collection of your best and worst experience in class, in school, and in life that you've written on paper so that later you can look back in that portfolio to see how you did on tests or what was happening in your life. This gives you the ability to improve your future.

I like it because I don't like seeing red marks on papers that I write. My Mom really likes it because she likes the idea of kids expressing themselves through writing and not coming home with marks on a paper the kid thought was good. I really like it.

8. The Interdisciplinary Connection

Before concluding this treatment of assessment portfolios to highlight the connections that can be made across the curriculum. The portfolio is without a doubt a powerful tool for any teacher in any subject. However, the real power behind the concept is not unleashed until teachers begin to use portfolios to link the knowledge and skills obtained in many areas of learning. A primary goal of education is the transfer of knowledge. If our students only learn and apply information in the isolation of specific subject areas our job is only half done. Portfolios are an excellent way to demonstrate how information from subject areas can be linked and transferred.

When reflecting on a variety of artifacts from many subjects that have been collected over a period of time, connections become clear. Students see how they use knowledge gained from one subject area to enhance their learning in others. They discover that strengths in one class can help them overcome weaknesses in another. It soon becomes apparent that life is filled with cross curricular connections, and in fact is fully integrated and whole.

There is no specific formula for creating an interdisciplinary photo album or portfolio. Instead there are as many ways as you and your colleagues can conceive. It begins with actually sitting down and thinking about what skills you are currently utilizing across the curriculum or which ones you need to begin highlighting. From there, decide on activities that will facilitate these interdisciplinary connections and could be included in a portfolio collection.

The character of any portfolio system will always reflect the students, subjects involved, teacher style, and space. In some cases the best thing to do is create a cross-subject portfolio. My team has done this in the form of a team portfolio that is monitored by the advisory teacher. We began this collection by inventorying the student's learning styles, multiple intelligences, and other key aspects of how each individual operates and learns. These collections are based on the concept that each person learns and processes information differently. After a learner profile has been created on each student we add a variety of artifacts that illustrate all the modalities of learning so students can monitor their progress and growth as learners.

Teachers can also create subject portfolios that include links to other classes. I maintain writing portfolios on my students, but whenever writing is used in other subject areas it is included in their English portfolio. This has not only helped the students to see how writing is a skill used in all classes, it also has helped to encourage other teachers to do more writing in their subject areas. Once the concept of transfer is integrated into your portfolio system it begins to mushroom with far-reaching effects.

The portfolios used in the parent conferences discussed in the previous chapter are also interdisciplinary in nature. Students are expected to keep examples of work from all classes in their collection. Like the portfolios kept on my team, these collections are monitored by the advisory teacher. This provides an excellent opportunity to include items illustrating the affective domain of the students' growth as well as their cognitive development.

If an integrated subject portfolio sounds like a little too much for you to tackle right now, try it for one unit. An interdisciplinary unit collection can not only be fun, it can help both teacher and students to find focus, meaning, and connections to the activities. There is no better way to show how all the tasks involved in your IDU are related – a primary purpose of such a unit. As always, have the students reflect on what they have learned, how they will use the information, what was the best part of the unit, and what they would do to improve the unit. This reflection will help them draw the needed conclusions about the knowledge gained and provide you with excellent feedback on what you can do to improve the unit if you repeat it. You might even get ideas for future educational experiences.

The portfolio is a valuable means of making interdisciplinary connections. Don't force it, but keep your eyes open for the natural connections that exist. Regardless of the vehicle used to facilitate it, the integration of learning is a major step toward developing lifelong learners. 🗁

A Teacher Reflects

Portfolios have become the foundation in my TAP, English, and reading classes. At first, I was apprehensive about using them because the process seemed to complicated; however, I was wrong! Portfolios are easy to implement and their uses are many. I use portfolios not only for student-chosen pieces of work, but for student-led conferences, grade analysis and graphing, self-assessment including goals, multiple intelligences, strengths, weaknesses, and various activities. I am completely sold on the importance and uses of portfolios in the classroom. I wouldn't have it any other way!!

9. Common Questions and Answers

This chapter covers some of the most common questions I am asked when discussing portfolios. It can serve as a summary and a review. There are many other questions, of course, but these answers combined with the preceding eight chapters should arm you well enough to institute portfolio assessment.

1. How can I be sure that portfolio assessment has the reliability and validity that my current way of grading does?

Portfolio assessment does not detract from or replace your current method of grading, it is meant to enhance it. You will still have to put grades in the grade book and on the report card. You will, however, be adding important dimensions to your evaluation. Properly used, portfolios actually increase your reliability and validity, because ample artifacts are available to back up your observations and conclusions.

2. Are grades and portfolios at cross purposes? Can they coexist peacefully?

By all means, grades and portfolios can work together peacefully. Utilizing a portfolio system of evaluation does not mean that you will stop giving grades – although you might wish you could. It does mean that you will begin to go beyond giving grades based primarily on test scores when assessing students' learning and progress. A major misconception about portfolios is the idea that they replace grades. Not so. Portfolios assessment is an important tool that makes it possible to assess informal as well as formal work that students do. Portfolios also provide a tool whereby students take on the responsibility of self-evaluation and bring deeper meaning to the assessment of student progress.

3. How much should be kept in a student portfolio?

There is no set number of artifacts that should be kept in the collection. Key considerations are keeping them manageable, space limitations, and maintaining a sufficient variety of the students' work to reflect their growth and progress. As long as you can deal with these factors, there is no such thing as too much or too little. As time goes on students can weed them out periodically, a process that brings on reflection and a consciousness of progress.

4. Are there things in the portfolio that you don't want students to see?

This is not a problem since portfolios are always accessible to students. The portfolio is not a place to keep any confidential item. Everything that goes into the collection should be suitable for the learner, the parents, and the teacher to view and should be completely understandable to them. In order for students to take part in their own evaluation they need to have access to all relevant information. There should be no secrets regarding how a student's final grade is determined.

5. What do you do if a student looses his or her portfolio?

This can indeed be a problem if it ever happens. The only thing that you can do in this case is to have that student begin a new collection and write a reflection of some sort that discusses what was in the lost portfolio and what he/she thought about that body of work. I have avoided this problem by never allowing the portfolio collection to leave the classroom. Some teachers, however, permit students to check them out.

6. Are portfolios maintained and passed on from year to year?

In an ideal world the student's collections of artifacts, or a portion of it, would follow the student from grade to grade. However, since most schools do not yet mandate a portfolio system, this can't happen. Other factors that can cause problems with this idea include the abundance of materials that would need to be maintained and passed on, as well as the reality that what is one teacher's treasure may be another teacher's trash. In many cases, the collection is greatly reduced at the end of the year to include only a previously determined selection of items that reflect certain learning objectives, and then it is passed on to the next teacher or kept by the student. I am presently investigating the concept of creating a data disk that could hold a great deal of material in a very small and manageable way. This system would incorporate the use of a scanner to put the work on the computer disk and cut down on data entry time.

7. What are some guidelines for weighting items that are put into the portfolio collection?

I believe teachers should weight an assignment at the time they give it. An assignment that goes into the collection is either graded and recorded before it goes in, or is assigned a work in progress grade that is proportionate with the task. Assessment portfolios should not require any changes in the way you currently weight your assignments.

8. Can a portfolio work in lab classes such as music or gym where there is little or no paperwork?

A photo album type collection would be a tremendous asset in such classes. When you are not recording written samples and tests, you end up with some very subjective observations on which to base the final grade. By utilizing a portfolio system you will have better evidence of the student's effort and progress over time. The twist is to use audio or video tapes and photographs to document students' learning. When you are able to observe the strides that learners have made you are in a much better position to place a judgment on their progress, and do not have to rely on your memory. Taping the students on several occasions throughout the year will also provide them with excellent opportunites to reflect on their progress and set goals for the future.

9. How does portfolio assessment fit in with district and state goals for student learning?

As is the case with any form of assessment that a teacher uses, portfolios should reflect the district and/or state outcomes and goals for learning. If teachers are assessing things unnecessarily, time and energy are being wasted. If teachers are aware of the objectives and the curriculum, and are clear about the district's beliefs and goals of evaluation, then their assessments will conform to the state and district goals. Portfolios don't require you to change all aspects of your system, they simply provide you with a place to keep measures and a vehicle for reflection. Keep in mind, however, that portfolios will help you develop significant skills and understandings that are probably not included in the more content-centered state or district outcomes.

10. Are portfolios being used for teacher evaluation?

The better question would be, why aren't they being used more? I can think of no better way for teachers to show their best side to an evaluator. The traditional classroom observation all too often becomes a show that doesn't really reflect the every day learning environment or touch the learnings that only develop over time. By utilizing a portfolio system a teacher can sit down with an evaluator and show the year at a glance via a variety of classroom artifacts. Classroom observations should not be eliminated completely, but they have been given undue importance. I am pleased to say that my district is now offering a portfolio option.

11. How does increasing technology fit into the use of assessment portfolios?

As schools continue to advance in technology, portfolios will be easier to maintain and pass on to other teachers than ever before. Student will be assigned a disk that will follow them as they pass from grade to grade. This disk can hold selected samples of the child's work in one subject area or from several classes. With a collection covering many years a clear picture of growth and progress will emerge. This system will allow the teacher to reflect on the student's work and evaluate the need to better individualize instruction. Using a disk will greatly reduce the space problems and will be far less problematic than passing fat folders from teacher to teacher. To further save time, a scanner can be used to input the work samples into the computer prior to saving them on the disk. This eliminates the need to type the work on a word processing program, and it allows for more versatility regarding the types of artifacts that are collected. ⌂

References

Clark, Mary E. (1991). *Portfolio assessment.* Boston: Houghton Mifflin

Farr, Roger (1991, June). Language Arts Assessment. Presentation at Naperville, IL.

Fletcher, Ralph.(1992, September). Writing Assessment. Presentation at Oak Park, IL.

Gardner, Howard (1993). *Multiple intelligences: The theory in practice.* New York: Basic Books

Guidelines for child's developmental progress portfolio. Early Prevention of School Failure, Peotone, IL, Author.

Smith, Inga H. (1992). *Portfolios: Linking instruction, learning, and assessment.* Evanston, IL: McDougal, Littell & Company.

Yancey, Kathleen B. (Ed.) (1992). *Portfolios in the writing classroom: An introduction.* Urbana, IL: National Council of Teachers of English.

NATIONAL MIDDLE SCHOOL ASSOCIATION

National Middle School Association was established in 1973 to serve as a voice for professionals and others interested in the education of young adolescents. The Association has grown rapidly and now enrolls members in all fifty states, the Canadian provinces, and forty-two other nations. In addition, fifty-three state, regional, and provincial middle school associations are official affiliates of NMSA.

NMSA is the only association dedicated exclusively to the education, development, and growth of young adolescents. Membership is open to all. While middle level teachers and administrators make up the bulk of the membership, central office personnel, college and university faculty, state department officials, other professionals, parents, and lay citizens are also actively involved in supporting our single mission – improving the educational experiences of 10-15 year olds. This open membership is a particular strength of NMSA.

The Association provides a variety of services, conferences, and materials in fulfilling its mission. In addition to *Middle School Journal*, the movement's premier professional journal, the Association publishes *Research in Middle Level Education Quarterly*, a wealth of books and monographs, videos, a general newsletter, an urban education newspaper, and occasional papers. The Association's highly acclaimed annual conference, which has drawn over 10,000 registrants in recent years, is held in the fall.

For information about NMSA and its many services contact the Headquarters at 2600 Corporate Exchange Drive, Suite 370, Columbus, Ohio 43231, TELEPHONE 800-528-NMSA, FAX 614-895-4750.